```
THIS BOOK BELONGS TO:
```

Important note: neither the publisher nor author of this book can be held responsible or liable for any damages, errors, losses or consequences that may result from a user using and storing information in this book.

Keep it in a safe and secure location and do not share your key, keywords or your passwords.

Treat it as carefully and sensitively as you would your passport or birth certificate.

If you travel with your book, it is advisable to keep a second master copy at home in the event that this book is lost or destroyed on travel.

Should this book get lost or misplaced or if someone has accessed it (despite its inbuilt security) it is recommended that you change all your passwords as soon as you can.

Using this book:

- 🔒 This is no ordinary book!
- 🔒 This book is designed to help you create and safely store your online passwords.
- 🔒 You could use it as a normal password log book; if you do, add the techniques at the back of the book to generate a strong password.
- 🔒 You can add a heightened/ increased layer of security by using the recommended key code to any written down passwords (see back of book) to help make it hack proof.
- 🔒 Ideally lock this book away in a safe or cabinet. Or else mix it in or between other books. It is intentionally of a slightly different size so it can be easily concealed

This book has been created for everyone to benefit from.

I lost all my passwords stored in my computer due to a hard drive failure. I came unstuck as without my passwords, and with no means of accessing them, I was unable to pass my own security.

I am also concerned about online data mining and hacking. Finally I decided to invest in a physical, hard copy password log book.

As each website has password requirements of differing length, symbols, numbers and special characters, it was impossible for me to remember them all. So I took this book with me where ever I went. Regrettably, I lost my password log book and with it all my banking sites, work, email, social networking passwords (to name just a few). My finances and my identity was potentially up for grabs. Worse still, once again I couldn't remember my passwords or data to log in or call and change them quickly to avoid hacking.

<u>So how could I safely store and remember all my passwords?</u>

*I decided to add a simple, quick, one minute encryption/ data scramble to protect myself so that **even if someone finds or accesses my book they cannot use my data.***

I am now less anxious when I travel and it provides me time to change any exposed information and I can still access my lost passwords by referring to my identical back-up copy at home.

I finally feel more comfortable storing my data in books again.

How to use this book:

- 🔒 Once you have come up with a secure, strong password (see recommendations on back pages on how to turn a simple password into a strong one); you then need to record it.

- 🔒 To code your password you will need to remember 1 key which will allow you to decrypt and encrypt all your stored passwords following the instructions at the back of the book.

- 🔒 You can create your own key or pick one from the 15 plus provided at the back of the book. No one can guess your key and this as well as a strong password (using the recommendations included) it will be very difficult/ near impossible to decode. Do not highlight or share your key!

- 🔒 You can also tear/cut out the encryption page from the end of the book for even further security once you know your keyword or number.

It may take a couple of minutes extra to get accustomed to encrypting but it will soon become second nature. It is also quite fun joining the world of cryptography!

- 🔒 Remember you need only encrypt your passwords or part of your passwords. You could also note down hints instead. The rest is noted as normal.

- 🔒 The remainder of the book is alphabetised for ease of retrieval with number of lettered pages available based on frequency of letter usage.

- 🔒 There is additional space to note and date stamp updated passwords as well as hints/ security questions.

- 🔒 There is a quick reference * slot at the end of the alphabetised list with a page for frequently used emails and updated passwords and an additional area to record information for your most frequently used/ favourite sites.

- 🔒 There is also a bonus page for software licenses and a few blank lined pages at the end to allow you to store any other important data such as Wi-Fi codes, home network settings, banking, computer and phone information etc..

Now turn to the back of the book for instructions on how to get started with recording in your Password Protected book. Enjoy!

A

🔒 Name/Reference:

🔒 Site Address:

🔒 Login ID/Username:

🔒 Date & Password:

🔒 Date & Password:

🔒 Hints, notes & security questions:

🔒 Name/Reference:

🔒 Site Address:

🔒 Login ID/Username:

🔒 Date & Password:

🔒 Date & Password:

🔒 Hints, notes & security questions:

🔒 Name/Reference:

🔒 Site Address:

🔒 Login ID/Username:

🔒 Date & Password:

🔒 Date & Password:

🔒 Hints, notes & security questions:

🔒 Name/Reference: _____ **A**

🔒 Site Address: _____

🔒 Login ID/Username: _____

🔒 Date & Password: _____

🔒 Date & Password: _____

🔒 Hints, notes & security questions: _____

_____

_____

🔒 Name/Reference: _____

🔒 Site Address: _____

🔒 Login ID/Username: _____

🔒 Date & Password: _____

🔒 Date & Password: _____

🔒 Hints, notes & security questions: _____

_____

_____

🔒 Name/Reference: _____

🔒 Site Address: _____

🔒 Login ID/Username: _____

🔒 Date & Password: _____

🔒 Date & Password: _____

🔒 Hints, notes & security questions: _____

_____

_____

A

🔒 Name/Reference:

🔒 Site Address:

🔒 Login ID/Username:

🔒 Date & Password:

🔒 Date & Password:

🔒 Hints, notes & security questions:

🔒 Name/Reference:

🔒 Site Address:

🔒 Login ID/Username:

🔒 Date & Password:

🔒 Date & Password:

🔒 Hints, notes & security questions:

🔒 Name/Reference:

🔒 Site Address:

🔒 Login ID/Username:

🔒 Date & Password:

🔒 Date & Password:

🔒 Hints, notes & security questions:

🔒 Name/Reference:

🔒 Site Address:

🔒 Login ID/Username:

🔒 Date & Password:

🔒 Date & Password:

🔒 Hints, notes & security questions:

🔒 Name/Reference:

🔒 Site Address:

🔒 Login ID/Username:

🔒 Date & Password:

🔒 Date & Password:

🔒 Hints, notes & security questions:

🔒 Name/Reference:

🔒 Site Address:

🔒 Login ID/Username:

🔒 Date & Password:

🔒 Date & Password:

🔒 Hints, notes & security questions:

B

- 🔒 Name/Reference:
- 🔒 Site Address:
- 🔒 Login ID/Username:
- 🔒 Date & Password:
- 🔒 Date & Password:
- 🔒 Hints, notes & security questions:

- 🔒 Name/Reference:
- 🔒 Site Address:
- 🔒 Login ID/Username:
- 🔒 Date & Password:
- 🔒 Date & Password:
- 🔒 Hints, notes & security questions:

- 🔒 Name/Reference:
- 🔒 Site Address:
- 🔒 Login ID/Username:
- 🔒 Date & Password:
- 🔒 Date & Password:
- 🔒 Hints, notes & security questions:

🔒 Name/Reference:

🔒 Site Address:

B

🔒 Login ID/Username:

🔒 Date & Password:

🔒 Date & Password:

🔒 Hints, notes & security questions:

🔒 Name/Reference:

🔒 Site Address:

🔒 Login ID/Username:

🔒 Date & Password:

🔒 Date & Password:

🔒 Hints, notes & security questions:

🔒 Name/Reference:

🔒 Site Address:

🔒 Login ID/Username:

🔒 Date & Password:

🔒 Date & Password:

🔒 Hints, notes & security questions:

B

- 🔒 Name/Reference:
- 🔒 Site Address:
- 🔒 Login ID/Username:
- 🔒 Date & Password:
- 🔒 Date & Password:
- 🔒 Hints, notes & security questions:

- 🔒 Name/Reference:
- 🔒 Site Address:
- 🔒 Login ID/Username:
- 🔒 Date & Password:
- 🔒 Date & Password:
- 🔒 Hints, notes & security questions:

- 🔒 Name/Reference:
- 🔒 Site Address:
- 🔒 Login ID/Username:
- 🔒 Date & Password:
- 🔒 Date & Password:
- 🔒 Hints, notes & security questions:

- 🔒 Name/Reference:
- 🔒 Site Address:
- 🔒 Login ID/Username:
- 🔒 Date & Password:
- 🔒 Date & Password:
- 🔒 Hints, notes & security questions:

- 🔒 Name/Reference:
- 🔒 Site Address:
- 🔒 Login ID/Username:
- 🔒 Date & Password:
- 🔒 Date & Password:
- 🔒 Hints, notes & security questions:

- 🔒 Name/Reference:
- 🔒 Site Address:
- 🔒 Login ID/Username:
- 🔒 Date & Password:
- 🔒 Date & Password:
- 🔒 Hints, notes & security questions:

C

- 🔒 Name/Reference:
- 🔒 Site Address:
- 🔒 Login ID/Username:
- 🔒 Date & Password:
- 🔒 Date & Password:
- 🔒 Hints, notes & security questions:

- 🔒 Name/Reference:
- 🔒 Site Address:
- 🔒 Login ID/Username:
- 🔒 Date & Password:
- 🔒 Date & Password:
- 🔒 Hints, notes & security questions:

- 🔒 Name/Reference:
- 🔒 Site Address:
- 🔒 Login ID/Username:
- 🔒 Date & Password:
- 🔒 Date & Password:
- 🔒 Hints, notes & security questions:

- 🔒 Name/Reference:
- 🔒 Site Address:
- 🔒 Login ID/Username:
- 🔒 Date & Password:
- 🔒 Date & Password:
- 🔒 Hints, notes & security questions:

- 🔒 Name/Reference:
- 🔒 Site Address:
- 🔒 Login ID/Username:
- 🔒 Date & Password:
- 🔒 Date & Password:
- 🔒 Hints, notes & security questions:

- 🔒 Name/Reference:
- 🔒 Site Address:
- 🔒 Login ID/Username:
- 🔒 Date & Password:
- 🔒 Date & Password:
- 🔒 Hints, notes & security questions:

C

- 🔒 Name/Reference:
- 🔒 Site Address:
- 🔒 Login ID/Username:
- 🔒 Date & Password:
- 🔒 Date & Password:
- 🔒 Hints, notes & security questions:

- 🔒 Name/Reference:
- 🔒 Site Address:
- 🔒 Login ID/Username:
- 🔒 Date & Password:
- 🔒 Date & Password:
- 🔒 Hints, notes & security questions:

- 🔒 Name/Reference:
- 🔒 Site Address:
- 🔒 Login ID/Username:
- 🔒 Date & Password:
- 🔒 Date & Password:
- 🔒 Hints, notes & security questions:

🔒 Name/Reference:

🔒 Site Address:

🔒 Login ID/Username:

🔒 Date & Password:

🔒 Date & Password:

🔒 Hints, notes & security questions:

🔒 Name/Reference:

🔒 Site Address:

🔒 Login ID/Username:

🔒 Date & Password:

🔒 Date & Password:

🔒 Hints, notes & security questions:

🔒 Name/Reference:

🔒 Site Address:

🔒 Login ID/Username:

🔒 Date & Password:

🔒 Date & Password:

🔒 Hints, notes & security questions:

D

- 🔒 Name/Reference:
- 🔒 Site Address:
- 🔒 Login ID/Username:
- 🔒 Date & Password:
- 🔒 Date & Password:
- 🔒 Hints, notes & security questions:

- 🔒 Name/Reference:
- 🔒 Site Address:
- 🔒 Login ID/Username:
- 🔒 Date & Password:
- 🔒 Date & Password:
- 🔒 Hints, notes & security questions:

- 🔒 Name/Reference:
- 🔒 Site Address:
- 🔒 Login ID/Username:
- 🔒 Date & Password:
- 🔒 Date & Password:
- 🔒 Hints, notes & security questions:

- 🔒 Name/Reference:
- 🔒 Site Address:
- 🔒 Login ID/Username:
- 🔒 Date & Password: Ⓓ
- 🔒 Date & Password:
- 🔒 Hints, notes & security questions:

- 🔒 Name/Reference:
- 🔒 Site Address:
- 🔒 Login ID/Username:
- 🔒 Date & Password:
- 🔒 Date & Password:
- 🔒 Hints, notes & security questions:

- 🔒 Name/Reference:
- 🔒 Site Address:
- 🔒 Login ID/Username:
- 🔒 Date & Password:
- 🔒 Date & Password:
- 🔒 Hints, notes & security questions:

D

- 🔒 Name/Reference:
- 🔒 Site Address:
- 🔒 Login ID/Username:
- 🔒 Date & Password:
- 🔒 Date & Password:
- 🔒 Hints, notes & security questions:

- 🔒 Name/Reference:
- 🔒 Site Address:
- 🔒 Login ID/Username:
- 🔒 Date & Password:
- 🔒 Date & Password:
- 🔒 Hints, notes & security questions:

- 🔒 Name/Reference:
- 🔒 Site Address:
- 🔒 Login ID/Username:
- 🔒 Date & Password:
- 🔒 Date & Password:
- 🔒 Hints, notes & security questions:

- 🔒 Name/Reference:
- 🔒 Site Address:
- 🔒 Login ID/Username:
- 🔒 Date & Password:
- 🔒 Date & Password:
- 🔒 Hints, notes & security questions:

- 🔒 Name/Reference:
- 🔒 Site Address:
- 🔒 Login ID/Username:
- 🔒 Date & Password:
- 🔒 Date & Password:
- 🔒 Hints, notes & security questions:

- 🔒 Name/Reference:
- 🔒 Site Address:
- 🔒 Login ID/Username:
- 🔒 Date & Password:
- 🔒 Date & Password:
- 🔒 Hints, notes & security questions:

- 🔒 Name/Reference:
- 🔒 Site Address:
- 🔒 Login ID/Username:
- 🔒 Date & Password:
- 🔒 Date & Password:
- 🔒 Hints, notes & security questions:

- 🔒 Name/Reference:
- 🔒 Site Address:
- 🔒 Login ID/Username:
- 🔒 Date & Password:
- 🔒 Date & Password:
- 🔒 Hints, notes & security questions:

- 🔒 Name/Reference:
- 🔒 Site Address:
- 🔒 Login ID/Username:
- 🔒 Date & Password:
- 🔒 Date & Password:
- 🔒 Hints, notes & security questions:

- 🔒 Name/Reference:
- 🔒 Site Address:
- 🔒 Login ID/Username:
- 🔒 Date & Password:
- 🔒 Date & Password:
- 🔒 Hints, notes & security questions:

- 🔒 Name/Reference:
- 🔒 Site Address:
- 🔒 Login ID/Username:
- 🔒 Date & Password:
- 🔒 Date & Password:
- 🔒 Hints, notes & security questions:

- 🔒 Name/Reference:
- 🔒 Site Address:
- 🔒 Login ID/Username:
- 🔒 Date & Password:
- 🔒 Date & Password:
- 🔒 Hints, notes & security questions:

- 🔒 Name/Reference:
- 🔒 Site Address:
- 🔒 Login ID/Username:
- 🔒 Date & Password:
- 🔒 Date & Password:
- 🔒 Hints, notes & security questions:

- 🔒 Name/Reference:
- 🔒 Site Address:
- 🔒 Login ID/Username:
- 🔒 Date & Password:
- 🔒 Date & Password:
- 🔒 Hints, notes & security questions:

- 🔒 Name/Reference:
- 🔒 Site Address:
- 🔒 Login ID/Username:
- 🔒 Date & Password:
- 🔒 Date & Password:
- 🔒 Hints, notes & security questions:

- 🔒 Name/Reference:
- 🔒 Site Address:
- 🔒 Login ID/Username:
- 🔒 Date & Password:
- 🔒 Date & Password:
- 🔒 Hints, notes & security questions:

- 🔒 Name/Reference:
- 🔒 Site Address:
- 🔒 Login ID/Username:
- 🔒 Date & Password:
- 🔒 Date & Password:
- 🔒 Hints, notes & security questions:

- 🔒 Name/Reference:
- 🔒 Site Address:
- 🔒 Login ID/Username:
- 🔒 Date & Password:
- 🔒 Date & Password:
- 🔒 Hints, notes & security questions:

🔒 Name/Reference:

🔒 Site Address:

🔒 Login ID/Username:

🔒 Date & Password:

🔒 Date & Password:

🔒 Hints, notes & security questions:

🔒 Name/Reference:

🔒 Site Address:

🔒 Login ID/Username:

🔒 Date & Password:

🔒 Date & Password:

🔒 Hints, notes & security questions:

🔒 Name/Reference:

🔒 Site Address:

🔒 Login ID/Username:

🔒 Date & Password:

🔒 Date & Password:

🔒 Hints, notes & security questions:

- 🔒 Name/Reference:
- 🔒 Site Address:
- 🔒 Login ID/Username:
- 🔒 Date & Password:
- 🔒 Date & Password:
- 🔒 Hints, notes & security questions:

F

- 🔒 Name/Reference:
- 🔒 Site Address:
- 🔒 Login ID/Username:
- 🔒 Date & Password:
- 🔒 Date & Password:
- 🔒 Hints, notes & security questions:

- 🔒 Name/Reference:
- 🔒 Site Address:
- 🔒 Login ID/Username:
- 🔒 Date & Password:
- 🔒 Date & Password:
- 🔒 Hints, notes & security questions:

- 🔒 Name/Reference:
- 🔒 Site Address:
- 🔒 Login ID/Username:
- 🔒 Date & Password:
- 🔒 Date & Password:
- 🔒 Hints, notes & security questions:

- 🔒 Name/Reference:
- 🔒 Site Address:
- 🔒 Login ID/Username:
- 🔒 Date & Password:
- 🔒 Date & Password:
- 🔒 Hints, notes & security questions:

- 🔒 Name/Reference:
- 🔒 Site Address:
- 🔒 Login ID/Username:
- 🔒 Date & Password:
- 🔒 Date & Password:
- 🔒 Hints, notes & security questions:

- 🔒 Name/Reference:
- 🔒 Site Address:
- 🔒 Login ID/Username:
- 🔒 Date & Password:
- 🔒 Date & Password:
- 🔒 Hints, notes & security questions:

F

- 🔒 Name/Reference:
- 🔒 Site Address:
- 🔒 Login ID/Username:
- 🔒 Date & Password:
- 🔒 Date & Password:
- 🔒 Hints, notes & security questions:

- 🔒 Name/Reference:
- 🔒 Site Address:
- 🔒 Login ID/Username:
- 🔒 Date & Password:
- 🔒 Date & Password:
- 🔒 Hints, notes & security questions:

- 🔒 Name/Reference:
- 🔒 Site Address:
- 🔒 Login ID/Username:
- 🔒 Date & Password:
- 🔒 Date & Password:
- 🔒 Hints, notes & security questions:

- 🔒 Name/Reference:
- 🔒 Site Address:
- 🔒 Login ID/Username:
- 🔒 Date & Password:
- 🔒 Date & Password:
- 🔒 Hints, notes & security questions:

- 🔒 Name/Reference:
- 🔒 Site Address:
- 🔒 Login ID/Username:
- 🔒 Date & Password:
- 🔒 Date & Password:
- 🔒 Hints, notes & security questions:

- 🔒 Name/Reference:
- 🔒 Site Address:
- 🔒 Login ID/Username:
- 🔒 Date & Password:
- 🔒 Date & Password:
- 🔒 Hints, notes & security questions:

- 🔒 Name/Reference:
- 🔒 Site Address:
- 🔒 Login ID/Username:
- 🔒 Date & Password:
- 🔒 Date & Password:
- 🔒 Hints, notes & security questions:

- 🔒 Name/Reference:
- 🔒 Site Address:
- 🔒 Login ID/Username:
- 🔒 Date & Password:
- 🔒 Date & Password:
- 🔒 Hints, notes & security questions:

- 🔒 Name/Reference:
- 🔒 Site Address:
- 🔒 Login ID/Username:
- 🔒 Date & Password:
- 🔒 Date & Password:
- 🔒 Hints, notes & security questions:

- 🔒 Name/Reference:
- 🔒 Site Address:
- 🔒 Login ID/Username:
- 🔒 Date & Password:
- 🔒 Date & Password:
- 🔒 Hints, notes & security questions:

- 🔒 Name/Reference:
- 🔒 Site Address:
- 🔒 Login ID/Username:
- 🔒 Date & Password:
- 🔒 Date & Password:
- 🔒 Hints, notes & security questions:

- 🔒 Name/Reference:
- 🔒 Site Address:
- 🔒 Login ID/Username:
- 🔒 Date & Password:
- 🔒 Date & Password:
- 🔒 Hints, notes & security questions:

Ⓖ

- 🔒 Name/Reference:
- 🔒 Site Address:
- 🔒 Login ID/Username:
- 🔒 Date & Password:
- 🔒 Date & Password:
- 🔒 Hints, notes & security questions:

- 🔒 Name/Reference:
- 🔒 Site Address:
- 🔒 Login ID/Username:
- 🔒 Date & Password:
- 🔒 Date & Password:
- 🔒 Hints, notes & security questions:

- 🔒 Name/Reference:
- 🔒 Site Address:
- 🔒 Login ID/Username:
- 🔒 Date & Password:
- 🔒 Date & Password:
- 🔒 Hints, notes & security questions:

H

- 🔒 Name/Reference:
- 🔒 Site Address:
- 🔒 Login ID/Username:
- 🔒 Date & Password:
- 🔒 Date & Password:
- 🔒 Hints, notes & security questions:

- 🔒 Name/Reference:
- 🔒 Site Address:
- 🔒 Login ID/Username:
- 🔒 Date & Password:
- 🔒 Date & Password:
- 🔒 Hints, notes & security questions:

- 🔒 Name/Reference:
- 🔒 Site Address:
- 🔒 Login ID/Username:
- 🔒 Date & Password:
- 🔒 Date & Password:
- 🔒 Hints, notes & security questions:

H

- 🔒 Name/Reference:
- 🔒 Site Address:
- 🔒 Login ID/Username:
- 🔒 Date & Password:
- 🔒 Date & Password:
- 🔒 Hints, notes & security questions:

- 🔒 Name/Reference:
- 🔒 Site Address:
- 🔒 Login ID/Username:
- 🔒 Date & Password:
- 🔒 Date & Password:
- 🔒 Hints, notes & security questions:

- 🔒 Name/Reference:
- 🔒 Site Address:
- 🔒 Login ID/Username:
- 🔒 Date & Password:
- 🔒 Date & Password:
- 🔒 Hints, notes & security questions:

H

- 🔒 Name/Reference:
- 🔒 Site Address:
- 🔒 Login ID/Username:
- 🔒 Date & Password:
- 🔒 Date & Password:
- 🔒 Hints, notes & security questions:

- 🔒 Name/Reference:
- 🔒 Site Address:
- 🔒 Login ID/Username:
- 🔒 Date & Password:
- 🔒 Date & Password:
- 🔒 Hints, notes & security questions:

- 🔒 Name/Reference:
- 🔒 Site Address:
- 🔒 Login ID/Username:
- 🔒 Date & Password:
- 🔒 Date & Password:
- 🔒 Hints, notes & security questions:

H

- 🔒 Name/Reference:
- 🔒 Site Address:
- 🔒 Login ID/Username:
- 🔒 Date & Password:
- 🔒 Date & Password:
- 🔒 Hints, notes & security questions:

- 🔒 Name/Reference:
- 🔒 Site Address:
- 🔒 Login ID/Username:
- 🔒 Date & Password:
- 🔒 Date & Password:
- 🔒 Hints, notes & security questions:

- 🔒 Name/Reference:
- 🔒 Site Address:
- 🔒 Login ID/Username:
- 🔒 Date & Password:
- 🔒 Date & Password:
- 🔒 Hints, notes & security questions:

- 🔒 Name/Reference:
- 🔒 Site Address:
- 🔒 Login ID/Username:
- 🔒 Date & Password:
- 🔒 Date & Password:
- 🔒 Hints, notes & security questions:

- 🔒 Name/Reference:
- 🔒 Site Address:
- 🔒 Login ID/Username:
- 🔒 Date & Password:
- 🔒 Date & Password:
- 🔒 Hints, notes & security questions:

- 🔒 Name/Reference:
- 🔒 Site Address:
- 🔒 Login ID/Username:
- 🔒 Date & Password:
- 🔒 Date & Password:
- 🔒 Hints, notes & security questions:

- 🔒 Name/Reference:
- 🔒 Site Address:
- 🔒 Login ID/Username:
- 🔒 Date & Password:
- 🔒 Date & Password:
- 🔒 Hints, notes & security questions:

- 🔒 Name/Reference:
- 🔒 Site Address:
- 🔒 Login ID/Username:
- 🔒 Date & Password:
- 🔒 Date & Password:
- 🔒 Hints, notes & security questions:

- 🔒 Name/Reference:
- 🔒 Site Address:
- 🔒 Login ID/Username:
- 🔒 Date & Password:
- 🔒 Date & Password:
- 🔒 Hints, notes & security questions:

- 🔒 Name/Reference:
- 🔒 Site Address:
- 🔒 Login ID/Username:
- 🔒 Date & Password:
- 🔒 Date & Password:
- 🔒 Hints, notes & security questions:

- 🔒 Name/Reference:
- 🔒 Site Address:
- 🔒 Login ID/Username:
- 🔒 Date & Password:
- 🔒 Date & Password:
- 🔒 Hints, notes & security questions:

- 🔒 Name/Reference:
- 🔒 Site Address:
- 🔒 Login ID/Username:
- 🔒 Date & Password:
- 🔒 Date & Password:
- 🔒 Hints, notes & security questions:

- 🔒 Name/Reference:
- 🔒 Site Address:
- 🔒 Login ID/Username:
- 🔒 Date & Password:
- 🔒 Date & Password:
- 🔒 Hints, notes & security questions:

- 🔒 Name/Reference:
- 🔒 Site Address:
- 🔒 Login ID/Username:
- 🔒 Date & Password:
- 🔒 Date & Password:
- 🔒 Hints, notes & security questions:

- 🔒 Name/Reference:
- 🔒 Site Address:
- 🔒 Login ID/Username:
- 🔒 Date & Password:
- 🔒 Date & Password:
- 🔒 Hints, notes & security questions:

J

- 🔒 Name/Reference:
- 🔒 Site Address:
- 🔒 Login ID/Username:
- 🔒 Date & Password:
- 🔒 Date & Password:
- 🔒 Hints, notes & security questions:

- 🔒 Name/Reference:
- 🔒 Site Address:
- 🔒 Login ID/Username:
- 🔒 Date & Password:
- 🔒 Date & Password:
- 🔒 Hints, notes & security questions:

- 🔒 Name/Reference:
- 🔒 Site Address:
- 🔒 Login ID/Username:
- 🔒 Date & Password:
- 🔒 Date & Password:
- 🔒 Hints, notes & security questions:

- 🔒 Name/Reference:
- 🔒 Site Address:
- 🔒 Login ID/Username:
- 🔒 Date & Password:
- 🔒 Date & Password:
- 🔒 Hints, notes & security questions:

- 🔒 Name/Reference:
- 🔒 Site Address:
- 🔒 Login ID/Username:
- 🔒 Date & Password:
- 🔒 Date & Password:
- 🔒 Hints, notes & security questions:

- 🔒 Name/Reference:
- 🔒 Site Address:
- 🔒 Login ID/Username:
- 🔒 Date & Password:
- 🔒 Date & Password:
- 🔒 Hints, notes & security questions:

J

- 🔒 Name/Reference:
- 🔒 Site Address:
- 🔒 Login ID/Username:
- 🔒 Date & Password:
- 🔒 Date & Password:
- 🔒 Hints, notes & security questions:

- 🔒 Name/Reference:
- 🔒 Site Address:
- 🔒 Login ID/Username:
- 🔒 Date & Password:
- 🔒 Date & Password:
- 🔒 Hints, notes & security questions:

- 🔒 Name/Reference:
- 🔒 Site Address:
- 🔒 Login ID/Username:
- 🔒 Date & Password:
- 🔒 Date & Password:
- 🔒 Hints, notes & security questions:

- 🔒 Name/Reference: J
- 🔒 Site Address:
- 🔒 Login ID/Username:
- 🔒 Date & Password:
- 🔒 Date & Password:
- 🔒 Hints, notes & security questions:

- 🔒 Name/Reference:
- 🔒 Site Address:
- 🔒 Login ID/Username:
- 🔒 Date & Password:
- 🔒 Date & Password:
- 🔒 Hints, notes & security questions:

- 🔒 Name/Reference:
- 🔒 Site Address:
- 🔒 Login ID/Username:
- 🔒 Date & Password:
- 🔒 Date & Password:
- 🔒 Hints, notes & security questions:

- 🔒 Name/Reference:
- 🔒 Site Address:
- 🔒 Login ID/Username:
- 🔒 Date & Password:
- 🔒 Date & Password:
- 🔒 Hints, notes & security questions:

- 🔒 Name/Reference:
- 🔒 Site Address:
- 🔒 Login ID/Username:
- 🔒 Date & Password:
- 🔒 Date & Password:
- 🔒 Hints, notes & security questions:

- 🔒 Name/Reference:
- 🔒 Site Address:
- 🔒 Login ID/Username:
- 🔒 Date & Password:
- 🔒 Date & Password:
- 🔒 Hints, notes & security questions:

- 🔒 Name/Reference:
- 🔒 Site Address:
- 🔒 Login ID/Username:
- 🔒 Date & Password:
- 🔒 Date & Password:
- 🔒 Hints, notes & security questions:

K

- 🔒 Name/Reference:
- 🔒 Site Address:
- 🔒 Login ID/Username:
- 🔒 Date & Password:
- 🔒 Date & Password:
- 🔒 Hints, notes & security questions:

- 🔒 Name/Reference:
- 🔒 Site Address:
- 🔒 Login ID/Username:
- 🔒 Date & Password:
- 🔒 Date & Password:
- 🔒 Hints, notes & security questions:

- 🔒 Name/Reference:
- 🔒 Site Address:
- 🔒 Login ID/Username:
- 🔒 Date & Password:
- 🔒 Date & Password:
- 🔒 Hints, notes & security questions:

- 🔒 Name/Reference:
- 🔒 Site Address:
- 🔒 Login ID/Username:
- 🔒 Date & Password:
- 🔒 Date & Password:
- 🔒 Hints, notes & security questions:

- 🔒 Name/Reference:
- 🔒 Site Address:
- 🔒 Login ID/Username:
- 🔒 Date & Password:
- 🔒 Date & Password:
- 🔒 Hints, notes & security questions:

- 🔒 Name/Reference:
- 🔒 Site Address:
- 🔒 Login ID/Username:
- 🔒 Date & Password:
- 🔒 Date & Password:
- 🔒 Hints, notes & security questions:

- 🔒 Name/Reference:
- 🔒 Site Address:
- 🔒 Login ID/Username:
- 🔒 Date & Password:
- 🔒 Date & Password:
- 🔒 Hints, notes & security questions:

- 🔒 Name/Reference:
- 🔒 Site Address:
- 🔒 Login ID/Username:
- 🔒 Date & Password:
- 🔒 Date & Password:
- 🔒 Hints, notes & security questions:

- 🔒 Name/Reference:
- 🔒 Site Address:
- 🔒 Login ID/Username:
- 🔒 Date & Password:
- 🔒 Date & Password:
- 🔒 Hints, notes & security questions:

- 🔒 Name/Reference:
- 🔒 Site Address:
- 🔒 Login ID/Username:
- 🔒 Date & Password:
- 🔒 Date & Password:
- 🔒 Hints, notes & security questions:

- 🔒 Name/Reference:
- 🔒 Site Address:
- 🔒 Login ID/Username:
- 🔒 Date & Password:
- 🔒 Date & Password:
- 🔒 Hints, notes & security questions:

- 🔒 Name/Reference:
- 🔒 Site Address:
- 🔒 Login ID/Username:
- 🔒 Date & Password:
- 🔒 Date & Password:
- 🔒 Hints, notes & security questions:

- 🔒 Name/Reference:
- 🔒 Site Address:
- 🔒 Login ID/Username:
- 🔒 Date & Password:
- 🔒 Date & Password:
- 🔒 Hints, notes & security questions:

- 🔒 Name/Reference:
- 🔒 Site Address:
- 🔒 Login ID/Username:
- 🔒 Date & Password:
- 🔒 Date & Password:
- 🔒 Hints, notes & security questions:

- 🔒 Name/Reference:
- 🔒 Site Address:
- 🔒 Login ID/Username:
- 🔒 Date & Password:
- 🔒 Date & Password:
- 🔒 Hints, notes & security questions:

- 🔒 Name/Reference:
- 🔒 Site Address:
- 🔒 Login ID/Username:
- 🔒 Date & Password:
- 🔒 Date & Password:
- 🔒 Hints, notes & security questions:

- 🔒 Name/Reference:
- 🔒 Site Address:
- 🔒 Login ID/Username:
- 🔒 Date & Password:
- 🔒 Date & Password:
- 🔒 Hints, notes & security questions:

- 🔒 Name/Reference:
- 🔒 Site Address:
- 🔒 Login ID/Username:
- 🔒 Date & Password:
- 🔒 Date & Password:
- 🔒 Hints, notes & security questions:

- 🔒 Name/Reference:
- 🔒 Site Address:
- 🔒 Login ID/Username:
- 🔒 Date & Password:
- 🔒 Date & Password:
- 🔒 Hints, notes & security questions:

- 🔒 Name/Reference:
- 🔒 Site Address:
- 🔒 Login ID/Username:
- 🔒 Date & Password:
- 🔒 Date & Password:
- 🔒 Hints, notes & security questions:

- 🔒 Name/Reference:
- 🔒 Site Address:
- 🔒 Login ID/Username:
- 🔒 Date & Password:
- 🔒 Date & Password:
- 🔒 Hints, notes & security questions:

- 🔒 Name/Reference:
- 🔒 Site Address:
- 🔒 Login ID/Username:
- 🔒 Date & Password:
- 🔒 Date & Password:
- 🔒 Hints, notes & security questions:

- 🔒 Name/Reference:
- 🔒 Site Address:
- 🔒 Login ID/Username:
- 🔒 Date & Password:
- 🔒 Date & Password:
- 🔒 Hints, notes & security questions:

- 🔒 Name/Reference:
- 🔒 Site Address:
- 🔒 Login ID/Username:
- 🔒 Date & Password:
- 🔒 Date & Password:
- 🔒 Hints, notes & security questions:

- 🔒 Name/Reference:
- 🔒 Site Address:
- 🔒 Login ID/Username:
- 🔒 Date & Password:
- 🔒 Date & Password:
- 🔒 Hints, notes & security questions:

- 🔒 Name/Reference:
- 🔒 Site Address:
- 🔒 Login ID/Username:
- 🔒 Date & Password:
- 🔒 Date & Password:
- 🔒 Hints, notes & security questions:

- 🔒 Name/Reference:
- 🔒 Site Address:
- 🔒 Login ID/Username:
- 🔒 Date & Password:
- 🔒 Date & Password:
- 🔒 Hints, notes & security questions:

- 🔒 Name/Reference:
- 🔒 Site Address:
- 🔒 Login ID/Username:
- 🔒 Date & Password:
- 🔒 Date & Password:
- 🔒 Hints, notes & security questions:

- 🔒 Name/Reference:
- 🔒 Site Address:
- 🔒 Login ID/Username:
- 🔒 Date & Password:
- 🔒 Date & Password:
- 🔒 Hints, notes & security questions:

- 🔒 Name/Reference:
- 🔒 Site Address:
- 🔒 Login ID/Username:
- 🔒 Date & Password:
- 🔒 Date & Password:
- 🔒 Hints, notes & security questions:

- 🔒 Name/Reference:
- 🔒 Site Address:
- 🔒 Login ID/Username:
- 🔒 Date & Password:
- 🔒 Date & Password:
- 🔒 Hints, notes & security questions:

- Name/Reference:
- Site Address:
- Login ID/Username:
- Date & Password:
- Date & Password:
- Hints, notes & security questions:

- Name/Reference:
- Site Address:
- Login ID/Username:
- Date & Password:
- Date & Password:
- Hints, notes & security questions:

- Name/Reference:
- Site Address:
- Login ID/Username:
- Date & Password:
- Date & Password:
- Hints, notes & security questions:

- 🔒 Name/Reference:
- 🔒 Site Address:
- 🔒 Login ID/Username:
- 🔒 Date & Password:
- 🔒 Date & Password:
- 🔒 Hints, notes & security questions:

- 🔒 Name/Reference:
- 🔒 Site Address:
- 🔒 Login ID/Username:
- 🔒 Date & Password:
- 🔒 Date & Password:
- 🔒 Hints, notes & security questions:

- 🔒 Name/Reference:
- 🔒 Site Address:
- 🔒 Login ID/Username:
- 🔒 Date & Password:
- 🔒 Date & Password:
- 🔒 Hints, notes & security questions:

🔒 Name/Reference:

🔒 Site Address:

🔒 Login ID/Username:

🔒 Date & Password:

🔒 Date & Password:

🔒 Hints, notes & security questions:

🔒 Name/Reference:

🔒 Site Address:

🔒 Login ID/Username:

🔒 Date & Password:

🔒 Date & Password:

🔒 Hints, notes & security questions:

🔒 Name/Reference:

🔒 Site Address:

🔒 Login ID/Username:

🔒 Date & Password:

🔒 Date & Password:

🔒 Hints, notes & security questions:

- 🔒 Name/Reference:
- 🔒 Site Address:
- 🔒 Login ID/Username:
- 🔒 Date & Password:
- 🔒 Date & Password:
- 🔒 Hints, notes & security questions:

- 🔒 Name/Reference:
- 🔒 Site Address:
- 🔒 Login ID/Username:
- 🔒 Date & Password:
- 🔒 Date & Password:
- 🔒 Hints, notes & security questions:

- 🔒 Name/Reference:
- 🔒 Site Address:
- 🔒 Login ID/Username:
- 🔒 Date & Password:
- 🔒 Date & Password:
- 🔒 Hints, notes & security questions:

- 🔒 Name/Reference:
- 🔒 Site Address:
- 🔒 Login ID/Username:
- 🔒 Date & Password:
- 🔒 Date & Password:
- 🔒 Hints, notes & security questions:

- 🔒 Name/Reference:
- 🔒 Site Address:
- 🔒 Login ID/Username:
- 🔒 Date & Password:
- 🔒 Date & Password:
- 🔒 Hints, notes & security questions:

- 🔒 Name/Reference:
- 🔒 Site Address:
- 🔒 Login ID/Username:
- 🔒 Date & Password:
- 🔒 Date & Password:
- 🔒 Hints, notes & security questions:

- 🔒 Name/Reference:
- 🔒 Site Address:
- 🔒 Login ID/Username:
- 🔒 Date & Password:
- 🔒 Date & Password:
- 🔒 Hints, notes & security questions:

- 🔒 Name/Reference:
- 🔒 Site Address:
- 🔒 Login ID/Username:
- 🔒 Date & Password:
- 🔒 Date & Password:
- 🔒 Hints, notes & security questions:

- 🔒 Name/Reference:
- 🔒 Site Address:
- 🔒 Login ID/Username:
- 🔒 Date & Password:
- 🔒 Date & Password:
- 🔒 Hints, notes & security questions:

- 🔒 Name/Reference:
- 🔒 Site Address:
- 🔒 Login ID/Username:
- 🔒 Date & Password:
- 🔒 Date & Password:
- 🔒 Hints, notes & security questions:

- 🔒 Name/Reference:
- 🔒 Site Address:
- 🔒 Login ID/Username:
- 🔒 Date & Password:
- 🔒 Date & Password:
- 🔒 Hints, notes & security questions:

- 🔒 Name/Reference:
- 🔒 Site Address:
- 🔒 Login ID/Username:
- 🔒 Date & Password:
- 🔒 Date & Password:
- 🔒 Hints, notes & security questions:

- 🔒 Name/Reference:
- 🔒 Site Address:
- 🔒 Login ID/Username:
- 🔒 Date & Password:
- 🔒 Date & Password:
- 🔒 Hints, notes & security questions:

- 🔒 Name/Reference:
- 🔒 Site Address:
- 🔒 Login ID/Username:
- 🔒 Date & Password:
- 🔒 Date & Password:
- 🔒 Hints, notes & security questions:

- 🔒 Name/Reference:
- 🔒 Site Address:
- 🔒 Login ID/Username:
- 🔒 Date & Password:
- 🔒 Date & Password:
- 🔒 Hints, notes & security questions:

🔒 Name/Reference:

🔒 Site Address:

🔒 Login ID/Username:

🔒 Date & Password:

🔒 Date & Password:

🔒 Hints, notes & security questions:

🔒 Name/Reference:

🔒 Site Address:

🔒 Login ID/Username:

🔒 Date & Password:

🔒 Date & Password:

🔒 Hints, notes & security questions:

🔒 Name/Reference:

🔒 Site Address:

🔒 Login ID/Username:

🔒 Date & Password:

🔒 Date & Password:

🔒 Hints, notes & security questions:

- 🔒 Name/Reference:
- 🔒 Site Address:
- 🔒 Login ID/Username:
- 🔒 Date & Password:
- 🔒 Date & Password:
- 🔒 Hints, notes & security questions:

- 🔒 Name/Reference:
- 🔒 Site Address:
- 🔒 Login ID/Username:
- 🔒 Date & Password:
- 🔒 Date & Password:
- 🔒 Hints, notes & security questions:

- 🔒 Name/Reference:
- 🔒 Site Address:
- 🔒 Login ID/Username:
- 🔒 Date & Password:
- 🔒 Date & Password:
- 🔒 Hints, notes & security questions:

- 🔒 Name/Reference:
- 🔒 Site Address:
- 🔒 Login ID/Username:
- 🔒 Date & Password:
- 🔒 Date & Password:
- 🔒 Hints, notes & security questions:

- 🔒 Name/Reference:
- 🔒 Site Address:
- 🔒 Login ID/Username:
- 🔒 Date & Password:
- 🔒 Date & Password:
- 🔒 Hints, notes & security questions:

P

- 🔒 Name/Reference:
- 🔒 Site Address:
- 🔒 Login ID/Username:
- 🔒 Date & Password:
- 🔒 Date & Password:
- 🔒 Hints, notes & security questions:

- 🔒 Name/Reference:
- 🔒 Site Address:
- 🔒 Login ID/Username:
- 🔒 Date & Password:
- 🔒 Date & Password:
- 🔒 Hints, notes & security questions:

- 🔒 Name/Reference:
- 🔒 Site Address:
- 🔒 Login ID/Username:
- 🔒 Date & Password:
- 🔒 Date & Password:
- 🔒 Hints, notes & security questions:

- 🔒 Name/Reference:
- 🔒 Site Address:
- 🔒 Login ID/Username:
- 🔒 Date & Password:
- 🔒 Date & Password:
- 🔒 Hints, notes & security questions:

- 🔒 Name/Reference:
- 🔒 Site Address:
- 🔒 Login ID/Username:
- 🔒 Date & Password:
- 🔒 Date & Password:
- 🔒 Hints, notes & security questions:

- 🔒 Name/Reference:
- 🔒 Site Address:
- 🔒 Login ID/Username:
- 🔒 Date & Password:
- 🔒 Date & Password:
- 🔒 Hints, notes & security questions:

- 🔒 Name/Reference:
- 🔒 Site Address:
- 🔒 Login ID/Username:
- 🔒 Date & Password:
- 🔒 Date & Password:
- 🔒 Hints, notes & security questions:

- 🔒 Name/Reference:
- 🔒 Site Address:
- 🔒 Login ID/Username:
- 🔒 Date & Password:
- 🔒 Date & Password:
- 🔒 Hints, notes & security questions:

- 🔒 Name/Reference:
- 🔒 Site Address:
- 🔒 Login ID/Username:
- 🔒 Date & Password:
- 🔒 Date & Password:
- 🔒 Hints, notes & security questions:

Q

- 🔒 Name/Reference:
- 🔒 Site Address:
- 🔒 Login ID/Username:
- 🔒 Date & Password:
- 🔒 Date & Password:
- 🔒 Hints, notes & security questions:

- 🔒 Name/Reference:
- 🔒 Site Address:
- 🔒 Login ID/Username:
- 🔒 Date & Password:
- 🔒 Date & Password:
- 🔒 Hints, notes & security questions:

- 🔒 Name/Reference:
- 🔒 Site Address:
- 🔒 Login ID/Username:
- 🔒 Date & Password:
- 🔒 Date & Password:
- 🔒 Hints, notes & security questions:

R

- 🔒 Name/Reference:
- 🔒 Site Address:
- 🔒 Login ID/Username:
- 🔒 Date & Password:
- 🔒 Date & Password:
- 🔒 Hints, notes & security questions:

- 🔒 Name/Reference:
- 🔒 Site Address:
- 🔒 Login ID/Username:
- 🔒 Date & Password:
- 🔒 Date & Password:
- 🔒 Hints, notes & security questions:

- 🔒 Name/Reference:
- 🔒 Site Address:
- 🔒 Login ID/Username:
- 🔒 Date & Password:
- 🔒 Date & Password:
- 🔒 Hints, notes & security questions:

R

- 🔒 Name/Reference:
- 🔒 Site Address:
- 🔒 Login ID/Username:
- 🔒 Date & Password:
- 🔒 Date & Password:
- 🔒 Hints, notes & security questions:

- 🔒 Name/Reference:
- 🔒 Site Address:
- 🔒 Login ID/Username:
- 🔒 Date & Password:
- 🔒 Date & Password:
- 🔒 Hints, notes & security questions:

- 🔒 Name/Reference:
- 🔒 Site Address:
- 🔒 Login ID/Username:
- 🔒 Date & Password:
- 🔒 Date & Password:
- 🔒 Hints, notes & security questions:

R

- 🔒 Name/Reference:
- 🔒 Site Address:
- 🔒 Login ID/Username:
- 🔒 Date & Password:
- 🔒 Date & Password:
- 🔒 Hints, notes & security questions:

- 🔒 Name/Reference:
- 🔒 Site Address:
- 🔒 Login ID/Username:
- 🔒 Date & Password:
- 🔒 Date & Password:
- 🔒 Hints, notes & security questions:

- 🔒 Name/Reference:
- 🔒 Site Address:
- 🔒 Login ID/Username:
- 🔒 Date & Password:
- 🔒 Date & Password:
- 🔒 Hints, notes & security questions:

R

- 🔒 Name/Reference:
- 🔒 Site Address:
- 🔒 Login ID/Username:
- 🔒 Date & Password:
- 🔒 Date & Password:
- 🔒 Hints, notes & security questions:

- 🔒 Name/Reference:
- 🔒 Site Address:
- 🔒 Login ID/Username:
- 🔒 Date & Password:
- 🔒 Date & Password:
- 🔒 Hints, notes & security questions:

- 🔒 Name/Reference:
- 🔒 Site Address:
- 🔒 Login ID/Username:
- 🔒 Date & Password:
- 🔒 Date & Password:
- 🔒 Hints, notes & security questions:

- 🔒 Name/Reference:
- 🔒 Site Address:
- 🔒 Login ID/Username:
- 🔒 Date & Password:
- 🔒 Date & Password:
- 🔒 Hints, notes & security questions:

- 🔒 Name/Reference:
- 🔒 Site Address:
- 🔒 Login ID/Username:
- 🔒 Date & Password:
- 🔒 Date & Password:
- 🔒 Hints, notes & security questions:

- 🔒 Name/Reference:
- 🔒 Site Address:
- 🔒 Login ID/Username:
- 🔒 Date & Password:
- 🔒 Date & Password:
- 🔒 Hints, notes & security questions:

- 🔒 Name/Reference:
- 🔒 Site Address:
- 🔒 Login ID/Username:
- 🔒 Date & Password:
- 🔒 Date & Password:
- 🔒 Hints, notes & security questions:

- 🔒 Name/Reference:
- 🔒 Site Address:
- 🔒 Login ID/Username:
- 🔒 Date & Password:
- 🔒 Date & Password:
- 🔒 Hints, notes & security questions:

- 🔒 Name/Reference:
- 🔒 Site Address:
- 🔒 Login ID/Username:
- 🔒 Date & Password:
- 🔒 Date & Password:
- 🔒 Hints, notes & security questions:

S

- 🔒 Name/Reference:
- 🔒 Site Address:
- 🔒 Login ID/Username:
- 🔒 Date & Password:
- 🔒 Date & Password:
- 🔒 Hints, notes & security questions:

- 🔒 Name/Reference:
- 🔒 Site Address:
- 🔒 Login ID/Username:
- 🔒 Date & Password:
- 🔒 Date & Password:
- 🔒 Hints, notes & security questions:

- 🔒 Name/Reference:
- 🔒 Site Address:
- 🔒 Login ID/Username:
- 🔒 Date & Password:
- 🔒 Date & Password:
- 🔒 Hints, notes & security questions:

- 🔒 Name/Reference:
- 🔒 Site Address:
- 🔒 Login ID/Username:
- 🔒 Date & Password:
- 🔒 Date & Password:
- 🔒 Hints, notes & security questions:

- 🔒 Name/Reference:
- 🔒 Site Address:
- 🔒 Login ID/Username:
- 🔒 Date & Password:
- 🔒 Date & Password:
- 🔒 Hints, notes & security questions:

- 🔒 Name/Reference:
- 🔒 Site Address:
- 🔒 Login ID/Username:
- 🔒 Date & Password:
- 🔒 Date & Password:
- 🔒 Hints, notes & security questions:

- 🔒 Name/Reference:
- 🔒 Site Address:
- 🔒 Login ID/Username:
- 🔒 Date & Password:
- 🔒 Date & Password:
- 🔒 Hints, notes & security questions:

- 🔒 Name/Reference:
- 🔒 Site Address:
- 🔒 Login ID/Username:
- 🔒 Date & Password:
- 🔒 Date & Password:
- 🔒 Hints, notes & security questions:

- 🔒 Name/Reference:
- 🔒 Site Address:
- 🔒 Login ID/Username:
- 🔒 Date & Password:
- 🔒 Date & Password:
- 🔒 Hints, notes & security questions:

- 🔒 Name/Reference:
- 🔒 Site Address:
- 🔒 Login ID/Username:
- 🔒 Date & Password:
- 🔒 Date & Password:
- 🔒 Hints, notes & security questions:

- 🔒 Name/Reference:
- 🔒 Site Address:
- 🔒 Login ID/Username:
- 🔒 Date & Password:
- 🔒 Date & Password:
- 🔒 Hints, notes & security questions:

- 🔒 Name/Reference:
- 🔒 Site Address:
- 🔒 Login ID/Username:
- 🔒 Date & Password:
- 🔒 Date & Password:
- 🔒 Hints, notes & security questions:

- 🔒 Name/Reference:
- 🔒 Site Address:
- 🔒 Login ID/Username:
- 🔒 Date & Password:
- 🔒 Date & Password:
- 🔒 Hints, notes & security questions:

- 🔒 Name/Reference:
- 🔒 Site Address:
- 🔒 Login ID/Username:
- 🔒 Date & Password:
- 🔒 Date & Password:
- 🔒 Hints, notes & security questions:

- 🔒 Name/Reference:
- 🔒 Site Address:
- 🔒 Login ID/Username:
- 🔒 Date & Password:
- 🔒 Date & Password:
- 🔒 Hints, notes & security questions:

- 🔒 Name/Reference:
- 🔒 Site Address:
- 🔒 Login ID/Username:
- 🔒 Date & Password:
- 🔒 Date & Password:
- 🔒 Hints, notes & security questions:

- 🔒 Name/Reference:
- 🔒 Site Address:
- 🔒 Login ID/Username:
- 🔒 Date & Password:
- 🔒 Date & Password:
- 🔒 Hints, notes & security questions:

- 🔒 Name/Reference:
- 🔒 Site Address:
- 🔒 Login ID/Username:
- 🔒 Date & Password:
- 🔒 Date & Password:
- 🔒 Hints, notes & security questions:

- 🔒 Name/Reference:
- 🔒 Site Address:
- 🔒 Login ID/Username:
- 🔒 Date & Password:
- 🔒 Date & Password:
- 🔒 Hints, notes & security questions:

- 🔒 Name/Reference:
- 🔒 Site Address:
- 🔒 Login ID/Username:
- 🔒 Date & Password:
- 🔒 Date & Password:
- 🔒 Hints, notes & security questions:

- 🔒 Name/Reference:
- 🔒 Site Address:
- 🔒 Login ID/Username:
- 🔒 Date & Password:
- 🔒 Date & Password:
- 🔒 Hints, notes & security questions:

- 🔒 Name/Reference:
- 🔒 Site Address:
- 🔒 Login ID/Username:
- 🔒 Date & Password:
- 🔒 Date & Password:
- 🔒 Hints, notes & security questions:

- 🔒 Name/Reference:
- 🔒 Site Address:
- 🔒 Login ID/Username:
- 🔒 Date & Password:
- 🔒 Date & Password:
- 🔒 Hints, notes & security questions:

- 🔒 Name/Reference:
- 🔒 Site Address:
- 🔒 Login ID/Username:
- 🔒 Date & Password:
- 🔒 Date & Password:
- 🔒 Hints, notes & security questions:

- 🔒 Name/Reference:
- 🔒 Site Address:
- 🔒 Login ID/Username:
- 🔒 Date & Password:
- 🔒 Date & Password:
- 🔒 Hints, notes & security questions:

- 🔒 Name/Reference:
- 🔒 Site Address:
- 🔒 Login ID/Username:
- 🔒 Date & Password:
- 🔒 Date & Password:
- 🔒 Hints, notes & security questions:

- 🔒 Name/Reference:
- 🔒 Site Address:
- 🔒 Login ID/Username:
- 🔒 Date & Password:
- 🔒 Date & Password:
- 🔒 Hints, notes & security questions:

- 🔒 Name/Reference:
- 🔒 Site Address:
- 🔒 Login ID/Username:
- 🔒 Date & Password:
- 🔒 Date & Password:
- 🔒 Hints, notes & security questions:

- 🔒 Name/Reference:
- 🔒 Site Address:
- 🔒 Login ID/Username:
- 🔒 Date & Password:
- 🔒 Date & Password:
- 🔒 Hints, notes & security questions:

- 🔒 Name/Reference:
- 🔒 Site Address:
- 🔒 Login ID/Username:
- 🔒 Date & Password:
- 🔒 Date & Password:
- 🔒 Hints, notes & security questions:

- 🔒 Name/Reference:
- 🔒 Site Address:
- 🔒 Login ID/Username:
- 🔒 Date & Password:
- 🔒 Date & Password:
- 🔒 Hints, notes & security questions:

- 🔒 Name/Reference:
- 🔒 Site Address:
- 🔒 Login ID/Username:
- 🔒 Date & Password:
- 🔒 Date & Password:
- 🔒 Hints, notes & security questions:

- 🔒 Name/Reference:
- 🔒 Site Address:
- 🔒 Login ID/Username:
- 🔒 Date & Password:
- 🔒 Date & Password:
- 🔒 Hints, notes & security questions:

- 🔒 Name/Reference:
- 🔒 Site Address:
- 🔒 Login ID/Username:
- 🔒 Date & Password:
- 🔒 Date & Password:
- 🔒 Hints, notes & security questions:

- 🔒 Name/Reference:
- 🔒 Site Address:
- 🔒 Login ID/Username:
- 🔒 Date & Password:
- 🔒 Date & Password:
- 🔒 Hints, notes & security questions:

- 🔒 Name/Reference:
- 🔒 Site Address:
- 🔒 Login ID/Username:
- 🔒 Date & Password:
- 🔒 Date & Password:
- 🔒 Hints, notes & security questions:

- 🔒 Name/Reference:
- 🔒 Site Address:
- 🔒 Login ID/Username:
- 🔒 Date & Password:
- 🔒 Date & Password:
- 🔒 Hints, notes & security questions:

- 🔒 Name/Reference:
- 🔒 Site Address:
- 🔒 Login ID/Username:
- 🔒 Date & Password:
- 🔒 Date & Password:
- 🔒 Hints, notes & security questions:

- 🔒 Name/Reference:
- 🔒 Site Address:
- 🔒 Login ID/Username:
- 🔒 Date & Password:
- 🔒 Date & Password:
- 🔒 Hints, notes & security questions:

- 🔒 Name/Reference:
- 🔒 Site Address:
- 🔒 Login ID/Username:
- 🔒 Date & Password:
- 🔒 Date & Password:
- 🔒 Hints, notes & security questions:

- 🔒 Name/Reference:
- 🔒 Site Address:
- 🔒 Login ID/Username:
- 🔒 Date & Password:
- 🔒 Date & Password:
- 🔒 Hints, notes & security questions:

- 🔒 Name/Reference:
- 🔒 Site Address:
- 🔒 Login ID/Username:
- 🔒 Date & Password:
- 🔒 Date & Password:
- 🔒 Hints, notes & security questions:

- 🔒 Name/Reference:
- 🔒 Site Address:
- 🔒 Login ID/Username:
- 🔒 Date & Password:
- 🔒 Date & Password:
- 🔒 Hints, notes & security questions:

- 🔒 Name/Reference:
- 🔒 Site Address:
- 🔒 Login ID/Username:
- 🔒 Date & Password:
- 🔒 Date & Password:
- 🔒 Hints, notes & security questions:

- 🔒 Name/Reference:
- 🔒 Site Address:
- 🔒 Login ID/Username:
- 🔒 Date & Password:
- 🔒 Date & Password:
- 🔒 Hints, notes & security questions:

- 🔒 Name/Reference:
- 🔒 Site Address:
- 🔒 Login ID/Username:
- 🔒 Date & Password:
- 🔒 Date & Password:
- 🔒 Hints, notes & security questions:

- 🔒 Name/Reference:
- 🔒 Site Address:
- 🔒 Login ID/Username:
- 🔒 Date & Password:
- 🔒 Date & Password:
- 🔒 Hints, notes & security questions:

- 🔒 Name/Reference:
- 🔒 Site Address:
- 🔒 Login ID/Username:
- 🔒 Date & Password:
- 🔒 Date & Password:
- 🔒 Hints, notes & security questions:

- 🔒 Name/Reference:
- 🔒 Site Address:
- 🔒 Login ID/Username:
- 🔒 Date & Password:
- 🔒 Date & Password:
- 🔒 Hints, notes & security questions:

🔒 Name/Reference:

🔒 Site Address:

🔒 Login ID/Username:

🔒 Date & Password:

🔒 Date & Password:

🔒 Hints, notes & security questions:

🔒 Name/Reference:

🔒 Site Address:

🔒 Login ID/Username:

🔒 Date & Password:

🔒 Date & Password:

🔒 Hints, notes & security questions:

🔒 Name/Reference:

🔒 Site Address:

🔒 Login ID/Username:

🔒 Date & Password:

🔒 Date & Password:

🔒 Hints, notes & security questions:

- 🔒 Name/Reference:
- 🔒 Site Address:
- 🔒 Login ID/Username:
- 🔒 Date & Password:
- 🔒 Date & Password:
- 🔒 Hints, notes & security questions:

- 🔒 Name/Reference:
- 🔒 Site Address:
- 🔒 Login ID/Username:
- 🔒 Date & Password:
- 🔒 Date & Password:
- 🔒 Hints, notes & security questions:

- 🔒 Name/Reference:
- 🔒 Site Address:
- 🔒 Login ID/Username:
- 🔒 Date & Password:
- 🔒 Date & Password:
- 🔒 Hints, notes & security questions:

- 🔒 Name/Reference:
- 🔒 Site Address:
- 🔒 Login ID/Username:
- 🔒 Date & Password:
- 🔒 Date & Password:
- 🔒 Hints, notes & security questions:

- 🔒 Name/Reference:
- 🔒 Site Address:
- 🔒 Login ID/Username:
- 🔒 Date & Password:
- 🔒 Date & Password:
- 🔒 Hints, notes & security questions:

- 🔒 Name/Reference:
- 🔒 Site Address:
- 🔒 Login ID/Username:
- 🔒 Date & Password:
- 🔒 Date & Password:
- 🔒 Hints, notes & security questions:

- 🔒 Name/Reference:
- 🔒 Site Address:
- 🔒 Login ID/Username:
- 🔒 Date & Password:
- 🔒 Date & Password:
- 🔒 Hints, notes & security questions:

- 🔒 Name/Reference:
- 🔒 Site Address:
- 🔒 Login ID/Username:
- 🔒 Date & Password:
- 🔒 Date & Password:
- 🔒 Hints, notes & security questions:

- 🔒 Name/Reference:
- 🔒 Site Address:
- 🔒 Login ID/Username:
- 🔒 Date & Password:
- 🔒 Date & Password:
- 🔒 Hints, notes & security questions:

Z

- 🔒 Name/Reference:
- 🔒 Site Address:
- 🔒 Login ID/Username:
- 🔒 Date & Password:
- 🔒 Date & Password:
- 🔒 Hints, notes & security questions:

- 🔒 Name/Reference:
- 🔒 Site Address:
- 🔒 Login ID/Username:
- 🔒 Date & Password:
- 🔒 Date & Password:
- 🔒 Hints, notes & security questions:

- 🔒 Name/Reference:
- 🔒 Site Address:
- 🔒 Login ID/Username:
- 🔒 Date & Password:
- 🔒 Date & Password:
- 🔒 Hints, notes & security questions:

Z

🔒 Date:

🔒 Email:

🔒 Password:

🔒 Date:

🔒 Email:

🔒 Password:

🔒 Date:

🔒 Email:

🔒 Password:

🔒 Date:

🔒 Email:

🔒 Password:

🔒 Date:

🔒 Email:

🔒 Password:

🔒 Date:

🔒 Email:

🔒 Password:

🔒 Date:

🔒 Email:

🔒 Password:

- 🔒 Software:
- 🔒 License No:
- 🔒 Purchase date:

- 🔒 Software:
- 🔒 License No:
- 🔒 Purchase date:

- 🔒 Software:
- 🔒 Licence No:
- 🔒 Purchase date:

- 🔒 Software:
- 🔒 License No:
- 🔒 Purchase date:

- 🔒 Software:
- 🔒 License No:
- 🔒 Purchase date:

- 🔒 Software:
- 🔒 License No:
- 🔒 Purchase date:

- 🔒 Software:
- 🔒 License No:
- 🔒 Purchase date:

Frequently used sites:

- 🔒 Name/Reference:
- 🔒 Site Address:
- 🔒 Login ID/Username:
- 🔒 Date & Password:
- 🔒 Date & Password:
- 🔒 Hints, notes & security questions:

- 🔒 Name/Reference:
- 🔒 Site Address:
- 🔒 Login ID/Username:
- 🔒 Date & Password:
- 🔒 Date & Password:
- 🔒 Hints, notes & security questions:

- 🔒 Name/Reference:
- 🔒 Site Address:
- 🔒 Login ID/Username:
- 🔒 Date & Password:
- 🔒 Date & Password:
- 🔒 Hints, notes & security questions:

Frequently used sites:

- 🔒 Name/Reference:
- 🔒 Site Address:
- 🔒 Login ID/Username:
- 🔒 Date & Password:
- 🔒 Date & Password:
- 🔒 Hints, notes & security questions:

- 🔒 Name/Reference:
- 🔒 Site Address:
- 🔒 Login ID/Username:
- 🔒 Date & Password:
- 🔒 Date & Password:
- 🔒 Hints, notes & security questions:

- 🔒 Name/Reference:
- 🔒 Site Address:
- 🔒 Login ID/Username:
- 🔒 Date & Password:
- 🔒 Date & Password:
- 🔒 Hints, notes & security questions:

103

105

Step 1: Make a strong password.

Below are some ways to make simple memorable passwords stronger and hacker resistant:

Note: the examples are just to illustrate the concepts being discussed.

- 🔒 The longer the password the harder it is to crack, it is recommended that passwords should be a minimum of 8 characters in length

- 🔒 Use a combination of upper case and lower case letters, characters, symbols and numbers.

- 🔒 Try not to use single words as passwords even translated ones.

- 🔒 Use random words to make a memorable sentence or image; blue Milk shop man blueMilkshopman.

- 🔒 Join words/ phrases together without spaces, you can use a hyphen – comma, colons, semi colons or special characters at certain intervals. E.g. a comma after 3rd character, a hyphen after 8th and exclamation last but 1, so bluemilkshopman becomes blu,eMilk-shopma!n. You can find your own preference.

- 🔒 Use symbols or numbers in place of letters e.g. @ in place of a; 0 in place of o, stronger still is (); 1 or ! In place of 'i' or 'l' e.g. Overtherainbow! becomes ()verther@1nb()w!

- 🔒 Try simply removing vowels in a password; Overtherainbow! would become vrthrnbw!

- 🔒 Try combining different techniques covered in this book; blueMilkshopman would be blM,lkshp-m!n if vowels are removed and then commas, hyphen and exclamation added.

If you write your information in soft pencil or erasable pen you can easily erase and update passwords to save re-writing everything when you change a password.

- Replace letters with phonic sounds such as f with ph or vice verse ph with f; My-Family would be My-Phmly or fat-Elephant would be pht-Lfnt etc..

- Think about applying SMS or txtspk where possible e.g. You Are A Great Mate can be changed to URAGr8M8

- Use z in place of s or vice verse e.g. The%Brown-Familie!s would be The%Brown-phamilie!z or ThB%rwnph-ml!z (if subsequently removing vowels)

- Avoid using family, pet names, address or date of births or any data that could be 'known' about you unless you apply some techniques to them.

- Consider spelling them backwards and inserting numbers and special characters in the middle; Rain8%bow would read wob%8naiR

- Try using the first letter of a memorable word phrase E.g.. I loved Paris in the summer of 89 would become ilPitso89

- If you added another technique from above it would be even stronger e.g. substituting letters to give !lP!ts()89

- Avoid number strings or letter strings such qwerty, abc, 123, 190670 or your car registrations.

- To log your written password just code the first and last letters or first 2 letters/ last 2 letters, note the remaining letters as stars but place any capitals, numbers or symbols e.g. C***%1*w

Avoid using the passwords given in the examples above.

Remember to change your logins and passwords frequently.

Never share your passwords with anyone, if you accidentally do change them immediately after.

Step 2: Encrypting your password or parts of it:

Create a substitution alphabet from a memorable keyword;

- 🔒 Write down the alphabet in order.

- 🔒 In the row below the alphabet write down your keyword (omitting duplicate letters – or pick a keyword with no repeated letters in it)

- 🔒 Continue filling this row with the remaining unused letters of the alphabet. See the example below where the keyword is 'keyword' it is then followed by the normal alphabet in order but with the letters from 'keyword' omitted.

- 🔒 If completed correctly all cells will be filled in. Use the top row to encrypt and the bottom row to decrypt back: e.g. KEYWORD using 'keyword' as key translates to FOXUJNW

A	B	C	D	E	F	G	H	I	J	K	L	M	N	O	P	Q	R	S	T	U	V	W	X	Y	Z
K	*E*	*Y*	*W*	*O*	*R*	*D*	A	B	C	F	G	H	I	J	L	M	N	P	Q	S	T	U	V	X	Z

A quicker method is a shift encryption but it is easier to crack however if only noting a couple of letters of a password will be just as good; just remember the number.

- 🔒 This method simply involves shifting the alphabet across a number and re-writing it on the bottom row.

- 🔒 You can shift the bottom row either backwards or forwards.

-2

A	B	C	D	E	F	G	H	I	J	K	L	M	N	O	P	Q	R	S	T	U	V	W	X	Y	Z
Y	Z	A	B	C	D	E	F	G	H	I	J	K	L	M	N	O	P	Q	R	S	T	U	V	W	X

- 🔒 Remember you do not need to code your entire password just a few letters (usually the first and last) put _ _ --- @@ or ** for the remaining letters and a hint.

- 🔒 You can pick from the keyword and shift tables on the next page or you can create your own (blank templates provided).

Keyword Encryption: (Choose from one of the following encryption/ decryption keywords, or make your own).

A	B	C	D	E	F	G	H	I	J	K	L	M	N	O	P	Q	R	S	T	U	V	W	X	Y	Z
K	E	Y	W	O	R	D	A	B	C	F	G	H	I	J	L	M	N	P	Q	S	T	U	V	X	Z

A	B	C	D	E	F	G	H	I	J	K	L	M	N	O	P	Q	R	S	T	U	V	W	X	Y	Z
R	A	I	N	B	O	W	C	D	E	F	G	H	J	K	L	M	P	Q	S	T	U	V	X	Y	Z

A	B	C	D	E	F	G	H	I	J	K	L	M	N	O	P	Q	R	S	T	U	V	W	X	Y	Z
H	O	L	I	D	A	Y	B	C	E	F	G	J	K	M	N	P	Q	R	S	T	U	V	W	X	Z

A	B	C	D	E	F	G	H	I	J	K	L	M	N	O	P	Q	R	S	T	U	V	W	X	Y	Z
C	O	M	P	L	E	X	A	B	D	F	G	H	I	J	K	N	Q	R	S	T	U	V	W	Y	Z

A	B	C	D	E	F	G	H	I	J	K	L	M	N	O	P	Q	R	S	T	U	V	W	X	Y	Z
F	R	O	Z	E	N	A	B	C	D	G	H	I	J	K	L	M	P	Q	S	T	U	V	W	X	Y

A	B	C	D	E	F	G	H	I	J	K	L	M	N	O	P	Q	R	S	T	U	V	W	X	Y	Z
T	O	P	G	U	N	A	B	C	D	E	F	H	I	J	K	L	M	Q	R	S	V	W	X	Y	Z

A	B	C	D	E	F	G	H	I	J	K	L	M	N	O	P	Q	R	S	T	U	V	W	X	Y	Z
C	O	M	P	U	T	E	R	A	B	D	F	G	H	I	J	K	L	N	Q	S	V	W	X	Y	Z

A	B	C	D	E	F	G	H	I	J	K	L	M	N	O	P	Q	R	S	T	U	V	W	X	Y	Z
E	X	O	T	I	C	A	B	D	F	G	H	J	K	L	M	N	P	Q	R	S	U	V	W	Y	Z

A	B	C	D	E	F	G	H	I	J	K	L	M	N	O	P	Q	R	S	T	U	V	W	X	Y	Z
Z	E	B	R	A	S	C	D	F	G	H	I	J	K	L	M	N	O	P	Q	T	U	V	W	X	Y

A	B	C	D	E	F	G	H	I	J	K	L	M	N	O	P	Q	R	S	T	U	V	W	X	Y	Z
Z	O	M	B	I	E	S	A	C	D	F	G	H	J	K	L	N	P	Q	R	T	U	V	W	X	Y

A	B	C	D	E	F	G	H	I	J	K	L	M	N	O	P	Q	R	S	T	U	V	W	X	Y	Z
L	O	V	E	D	A	B	C	F	G	H	I	J	K	M	N	P	Q	R	S	T	U	W	X	Y	Z

A	B	C	D	E	F	G	H	I	J	K	L	M	N	O	P	Q	R	S	T	U	V	W	X	Y	Z
P	O	W	E	R	F	U	L	A	B	C	D	G	H	I	J	K	M	N	Q	S	T	V	X	Y	Z

Shift Encryption

-2

A	B	C	D	E	F	G	H	I	J	K	L	M	N	O	P	Q	R	S	T	U	V	W	X	Y	Z
Y	Z	A	B	C	D	E	F	G	H	I	J	K	L	M	N	O	P	Q	R	S	T	U	V	W	X

-4

A	B	C	D	E	F	G	H	I	J	K	L	M	N	O	P	Q	R	S	T	U	V	W	X	Y	Z
W	X	Y	Z	A	B	C	D	E	F	G	H	I	J	K	L	M	N	O	P	Q	R	S	T	U	V

+3

A	B	C	D	E	F	G	H	I	J	K	L	M	N	O	P	Q	R	S	T	U	V	W	X	Y	Z
D	E	F	G	H	I	J	K	L	M	N	O	P	Q	R	S	T	U	V	W	X	Y	Z	A	B	C

+5

A	B	C	D	E	F	G	H	I	J	K	L	M	N	O	P	Q	R	S	T	U	V	W	X	Y	Z
F	G	H	I	J	K	L	M	N	O	P	Q	R	S	T	U	V	W	X	Y	Z	A	B	C	D	E

Own Encryption

A	B	C	D	E	F	G	H	I	J	K	L	M	N	O	P	Q	R	S	T	U	V	W	X	Y	Z

A	B	C	D	E	F	G	H	I	J	K	L	M	N	O	P	Q	R	S	T	U	V	W	X	Y	Z

A	B	C	D	E	F	G	H	I	J	K	L	M	N	O	P	Q	R	S	T	U	V	W	X	Y	Z

A	B	C	D	E	F	G	H	I	J	K	L	M	N	O	P	Q	R	S	T	U	V	W	X	Y	Z

A	B	C	D	E	F	G	H	I	J	K	L	M	N	O	P	Q	R	S	T	U	V	W	X	Y	Z

A	B	C	D	E	F	G	H	I	J	K	L	M	N	O	P	Q	R	S	T	U	V	W	X	Y	Z

✂ Cut this page out if you prefer as you can now create your own encryption and decryption tables where ever you are.

Printed in Dunstable, United Kingdom